Use of English

Five practice tests for the **Cambridge B2 First + bonus tests**

Dominika Zając

PROSPERITY EDUCATION
www.prosperityeducation.net

Registered offices: Sherlock Close, Cambridge
CB3 0HP, United Kingdom

© Prosperity Education Ltd. 2024

First published 2024

ISBN: 978-1-915654-20-5

This publication is in copyright. Subject to statutory exception and to the provisions of relevant collective licensing agreements, no reproduction of any part may take place without the written permission of Prosperity Education.

'Use of English', 'Cambridge B2 First' and 'FCE' are brands belonging to The Chancellor, Masters and Scholars of the University of Cambridge and are not associated with Prosperity Education or its products.

Cover design and typesetting by ORP Cambridge

For further information and resources, visit:
www.prosperityeducation.net

To infinity and beyond.

Contents

Introduction	2
About the Cambridge B2 First exam	3
Test 1	5
Test 2	13
Test 3	21
Test 4	29
Test 5	37
Answer key – Test 1	46
Answer key – Test 2	47
Answer key – Test 3	48
Answer key – Test 4	49
Answer key – Test 5	50

Bonus material

B2 First Reading – Test 1	53
B2 First Reading – Test 2	61
B2 First Reading – Test 3	69
B2 First Use of English – Test 1	77
B2 First Use of English – Test 2	85
B2 First Use of English – Test 3	93

Introduction

Welcome to this third edition of sample tests for the Cambridge B2 First (FCE), Use of English examination (Parts 1–4).

The pass threshold of the Cambridge B2 First (FCE) is 60%, and so, in order to allow ample time for the Reading parts (Parts 5–7) of Paper 1, it is advisable that candidates complete The Use of English section (Parts 1–4) as quickly as possible while maintaining accuracy. For instance, completing each part in fewer than five minutes will allow 55 minutes in which to complete the Reading parts.

This resource comprises five whole Use of English tests, answer keys, write-in answer sheets and a marking scheme, allowing you to score each test out of 36 marks. In addition, six Reading and Use of English tests, taken from our popular Cambridge resources, are included as **bonus material**.

The content has been written to closely replicate the Cambridge exam experience, and has undergone comprehensive expert and peer review. You or your students, if you are a teacher, will hopefully enjoy the wide range of essay topics and benefit from the repetitive practice, something that is key to preparing for this part of the B2 First (FCE) examination.

We hope that you will find this resource a useful study aid, and we wish you all the best in preparing for the exam.

Prosperity Education
Cambridge, 2024

Dominika Zając is an English examiner for both the Matura and eighth-grade exams in Poland, and has taught English for more than 20 years. She is the co-author of textbooks *New Enterprise* and *4Minds* by Express Publishing (2019), and *Angielski Słowo do Słowa* by Edgard (2024).

For more Cambridge exam-preparation materials, including free sample tests and online resources, visit www.prosperityeducation.net

About the B2 First exam

The Use of English section of the B2 First (FCE) examination is broken down into four parts:

Part 1. Multiple choice cloze	
What is being tested?	This part of the exam mostly tests vocabulary, idioms, collocations, shades of meaning, phrasal verbs, complementation, semantic precision and fixed phrases.
How does it work?	It contains a test with eight gaps, each gap prompting multiple-choice questions. Each question has four possible answers, only one of which is correct.
How is it marked?	One mark is awarded for each correct answer.

Part 2. Open cloze	
What is being tested?	This part of the exam has a lexico-grammatical focus, testing candidates' awareness and control of grammar, fixed phrasing, collocation, semantic precision and, to an extent, vocabulary (the particles/prepositions for phrasal verbs).
How does it work?	It contains a text with eight gaps, each gap representing a missing word. No hints are given: candidates must think of the correct word for each gap.
How is it marked?	One mark is awarded for each correct answer.

Part 3. Word formation	
What is being tested?	This part of the exam focuses on affixation, internal changes and compounding in word formation, and vocabulary.
How does it work?	It contains a text with eight gaps, each gap representing a missing word. Beside each gap is a 'prompt' word that must be altered in some way to complete the sentence correctly.
How is it marked?	One mark is awarded for each correct answer.

Part 4. Key word transformation	
What is being tested?	This part of the exam has a lexico-grammatical focus, testing lexis, grammar and vocabulary.
How does it work?	It contains six sentences, each followed by a 'key' word and an alternative sentence conveying the same meaning as the first but with a gap in the middle. Candidates are to use the keyword provided to complete the second sentence so that it has a similar meaning to the first sentence. Candidates cannot change the keyword provided.
How is it marked?	Each correct answer is broken down into two marks.

Prosperity Education Ltd.
Cambridge, CB3 0HP
United Kingdom

Dear Customer,

Thank you for buying from us.

As an independent publisher, we would really appreciate it if you would leave us your honest feedback.

	Happy with your purchase? Simply log in to your Amazon account to leave a review.	
	Not happy? Please reach out to our support team: admin@prosperityeducation.net	

If you like our resources and what we do, please help us get our story out there.

	You can follow Prosperity Education (and in fact any of your favourite authors) on **Amazon**.	
	Our **website** contains lots of free exam-practice materials and sample downloads.	
	Our **Facebook** page regularly posts English language quizzes, discount codes and free stuff.	
	Follow our **Instagram** stories for updates on our English teaching and learning resources.	
	Subscribe to our **Youtube** channel for Listening, Speaking and Writing practice and tutorials.	

I wish you all the very best for your studies.

Tom O'Reilly, Founder of Prosperity Education

PS. This resource is also available as **a PDF download** from www.prosperityeducation.net
Enter the code 10PERCENTPDF at checkout for 10% off.

Cambridge B2 First Use of English

Test 1

Cambridge B2 First Use of English

Part 1

For questions 1–8, read the text below and decide which answer best fits each gap. In the separate answer sheet, mark the appropriate answer (A, B, C or D).

Exploring Lisbon

Lisbon, or *Lisboa*, is the capital and also the biggest city of Portugal. It is known **(1)**_____ its beautiful location on the seven hills by the River Tagus.

Its city centre is small and compact, so you can **(2)**_____ walk everywhere or take the famous tram 28 to see the sights. There are many interesting things to do in Lisbon and lots of landmarks to see, **(3)**_____ the Jeronimos Monastery in Belem or the popular Commerce Plaza.

One of the must-visit attractions in Lisbon is the historic district of Alfama where you can **(4)**_____ lost in the maze of narrow streets. Don't forget to take a stroll to the Sao Jorge Castle, where, standing at the top of the hill, you'll be able to **(5)**_____ the views of the city.

In the evenings, you can **(6)**_____ time listening to *Fado* music in one of the city's traditional restaurants. If you feel like eating something really delicious, **(7)**_____ to the bustling Mercado da Riberia to sample local delicacies, such as *pastel de nata*.

Whatever you decide to do, don't **(8)**_____ to a rigid plan. Just enjoy yourself and have the time of your life.

1	A	about	B	of	C	for	D	with
2	A	either	B	also	C	both	D	as well
3	A	similar to	B	for instance	C	as for	D	just like
4	A	be	B	get	C	have	D	bring
5	A	observe	B	examine	C	look	D	admire
6	A	waste	B	pass	C	spend	D	lose
7	A	head	B	lead	C	get	D	direct
8	A	fasten	B	attach	C	stick	D	fix

Part 2

For questions 9–16, read the text below and decide which word best fits each gap. Use only one word for each gap. In the separate answer sheet, write your answers in capital letters, using one box per letter.

Living in the Digital Age

The way we communicate has been hugely transformed **(9)**_____ the digital age we live in.

Emails, social media and instant messaging enable us **(10)**_____ connect with people all over the world at anytime. However, the possibility of being constantly connected has **(11)**_____ presented some challenges. For example, an excessive use of smartphones can lead to addiction **(12)**_____ can be harmful to our health.

The internet has also changed the ways in which we work. Many jobs can now **(13)**_____ done remotely, allowing employees to work comfortably from their homes. Although there are many supporters of this way of working, the trend has raised concerns such as its impact on work-life balance and the future of traditional workplaces, **(14)**_____ others.

Apart from these issues, there are also risks associated with illegal online activities, such as hacking or identity theft, which we need to **(15)**_____ into account and try to protect ourselves against.

In conclusion, we can't deny that technology has influenced our lives in many positive ways, but it is important to keep **(16)**_____ with its development and to know how to use it responsibly.

Cambridge B2 First Use of English

Part 3

For questions 17–24, use the stem word on the right to form the correct word that fills each gap. In the separate answer sheet, write your answers in capital letters, using one box per letter.

There is no success without failure

Dealing with failure is part and parcel of everyday life, which is why we should know how to react to it.

When we are faced with an (17)_____ problem, it's natural to feel frustrated or even overwhelmed. In these instances, we should learn how to respond (18)_____ to a situation and remember that experiencing failure is not the end of the world. We should rather treat it as an opportunity for development and (19)_____.

EXPECT

ADEQUATE

IMPROVE

First of all, it's not a good idea to blame our misfotunes on others or external factors. Instead, we should take responsibility for our (20)_____ because failure is often a result of our own decisions. We should analyse what went wrong and try to learn from our mistakes. This can help us to develop (21)_____ and adaptability.

ACT

STRONG

Although it may seem (22)_____ at first, failure can lead to success in the long run. If you want to achieve your best and accomplish (23)_____ things, you shouldn't be afraid of making mistakes along the way. They are just an (24)_____ part of our lives. Remember, there is no success without failure.

LIKE

ORDINARY

AVOID

Part 4

For questions 25–30, complete the second sentence, using the word given, so that it has a similar meaning to the first sentence. Do not change the word provided and use between two and five words in total. In the separate answer sheet, write your answers in capital letters, using one box per letter.

25 We had to postpone the meeting until the following week.
    OFF
    The meeting _____ until the following week.

26 I last saw Peter a long time ago.
    NOT
    I _____ a long time.

27 Although he was ill, he went to school.
    SPITE
    _____, he went to school.

28 My flat is being redecorated right now.
    HAVING
    I _____ right now.

29 I think you should talk to Susan.
    IF
    _____, I would talk to Susan.

30 Buying so much food wasn't necessary.
    NEED
    We _____ so much food.

Answer sheet: Cambridge B2 First
Use of English

Test No. ☐

Mark out of 36 ☐

Name _____   **Date** _____

Part 1: Multiple choice   8 marks

Mark the appropriate answer (A, B, C or D).

0 A **B** C D

1 A B C D   5 A B C D
2 A B C D   6 A B C D
3 A B C D   7 A B C D
4 A B C D   8 A B C D

Part 2: Open cloze   8 marks

Write your answers in capital letters, using one box per letter.

0 | B | E | C | A | U | S | E |

9
10
11
12
13
14
15
16

Part 3: Word formation

8 marks

Write your answers in capital letters, using one box per letter.

17.
18.
19.
20.
21.
22.
23.
24.

Part 4: Key word transformation

12 marks

Write your answers in capital letters, using one box per letter.

25.
26.
27.
28.
29.
30.

Cambridge B2 First Use of English

Test 2

Cambridge B2 First Use of English

Part 1

For questions 1–8, read the text below and decide which answer best fits each gap. In the separate answer sheet, mark the appropriate answer (A, B, C or D).

The importance of physical exercise

Everybody knows that **(1)**_____ in shape is extremely important if we want to be healthy and look good. **(2)**_____, you should remember to do it properly to avoid injuries.

The first thing you should **(3)**_____ in mind is the type of exercise that would be most suitable for you. If you like the company of other people, for instance, consider engaging **(4)**_____ a team sport. This may **(5)**_____ the bull's eye and become your favourite pastime. However, if you are more of a private person, you may enjoy jogging or cycling. Alternatively, you may opt **(6)**_____ workouts at the gym or participate in fitness classes. The obvious advantage of attending a fitness centre is the fact that it can be done **(7)**_____ of weather conditions. If you are more adventurous, you could try martial arts, which not only improve your fitness level **(8)**_____ also develop your self-defence skills.

Whatever activity you decide on, it'll be better than leading a sedentary lifestyle.

Good luck!

1	A	holding	B	feeling	C	having	D	staying
2	A	Nevertheless	B	Since	C	Accordingly	D	Meanwhile
3	A	carry	B	bring	C	bear	D	put
4	A	up	B	in	C	on	D	at
5	A	hit	B	shoot	C	score	D	achieve
6	A	at	B	on	C	for	D	in
7	A	besides	B	instead	C	despite	D	regardless
8	A	but	B	or	C	and	D	while

Part 2

For questions 9–16, read the text below and decide which word best fits each gap. Use only one word for each gap. In the separate answer sheet, write your answers in capital letters, using one box per letter.

Small steps to make a big difference

Looking at the changes in our planet's climate and the ecological threats we face, it is not surprising that environmental issues have been widely discussed in recent years.

Ecologists often claim that unless we take care of the environment, we will be to blame **(9)**_____ its bleak future. The good news is that there are several things that we can do regarding this issue, and they **(10)**_____ not be overly challenging. For instance, **(11)**_____ small changes in our daily lives might be enough.

First of all, when purchasing groceries we could protect the environment as **(12)**_____ as we opt for reusable bags rather than plastic ones or select products with reduced packaging. Another way to keep our environment clean is **(13)**_____ sort through rubbish and put recyclable products in the correct bins. This would allow us to reuse a greater **(14)**_____ of items and prevent them from ending up in landfills.

Using public transport or 'carpooling' (sharing car journeys with other people) also has a positive influence **(15)**_____ our environment. It helps to improve the quality of air and reduces traffic congestion, **(16)**_____ in turn can make people healthier and less stressed.

In summary, taking simple steps like these can help preserve our environment for future generations.

Part 3

For questions 17–24, use the stem word on the right to form the correct word that fills each gap. In the separate answer sheet, write your answers in capital letters, using one box per letter.

Did we have lives before mobile phones?

Nowadays, people can't imagine their lives without their beloved mobile phones, which accompany them everywhere. But have you ever taken into **(17)**_____ how it all began? — **CONSIDER**

The person who is responsible for this is Martin Cooper, and it wouldn't be an **(18)**_____ to say that he has revolutionised the ways in which people communicate. — **EXAGGERATE**

However, the evolution that mobile phones have undergone within the last decades is quite **(19)**_____. The first phone, affectionately remembered as 'The Brick', was massive and weighed a lot, but it was considered **(20)**_____ at the time. — **REMARK** / **REVOLUTION**

For the first commercial, portable phone, introduced in 1983 by Motorola, consumers had to pay a **(21)**_____ sum of money: $4,000. Its battery lasted only 30 minutes and took 10 hours to charge. **(22)**_____, it could only be used for voice communication. — **SUBSTANCE** / **ADDITION**

The phones we have now are very different to those in the 1980s. They have not only changed a lot in their **(23)**_____ design, but they can also do many things at once. They have replaced the need for separate cameras, music players and even computers. I wonder if they are already perfect or whether there is still some room for **(24)**_____. — **PHYSICS** / **IMPROVE**

We'll see what the future holds for us.

Test 2

Part 4

For questions 25–30, complete the second sentence, using the word given, so that it has a similar meaning to the first sentence. Do not change the word provided and use between two and five words in total. In the separate answer sheet, write your answers in capital letters, using one box per letter.

25 It was so loud that I could hardly hear her.
    DIFFICULTY
    It was so loud that _____ her.

26 I hate it when you make so much noise.
    WISH
    I _____ making so much noise.

27 Perhaps she didn't break her leg.
    MAY
    She _____ her leg.

28 I'm going to finish watching this series by the end of this week.
    WATCHED
    I _____ this series by the end of this week.

29 "You lied to me again," Jessica said to Mark.
    OF
    Jessica _____ to her.

30 "I won't be late again," said Tom.
    PROMISED
    Tom _____ late again.

Answer sheet: Cambridge B2 First
Use of English

Test No. ☐

Mark out of 36 ☐

Name _____   Date _____

Part 1: Multiple choice   8 marks

Mark the appropriate answer (A, B, C or D).

0 A **B** C D

1	A B C D	5	A B C D
2	A B C D	6	A B C D
3	A B C D	7	A B C D
4	A B C D	8	A B C D

Part 2: Open cloze   8 marks

Write your answers in capital letters, using one box per letter.

0 B E C A U S E

9 ☐☐☐☐☐☐☐☐☐☐
10 ☐☐☐☐☐☐☐☐☐☐
11 ☐☐☐☐☐☐☐☐☐☐
12 ☐☐☐☐☐☐☐☐☐☐
13 ☐☐☐☐☐☐☐☐☐☐
14 ☐☐☐☐☐☐☐☐☐☐
15 ☐☐☐☐☐☐☐☐☐☐
16 ☐☐☐☐☐☐☐☐☐☐

Part 3: Word formation

8 marks

Write your answers in capital letters, using one box per letter.

17.
18.
19.
20.
21.
22.
23.
24.

Part 4: Key word transformation

12 marks

Write your answers in capital letters, using one box per letter.

25.
26.
27.
28.
29.
30.

Cambridge B2 First Use of English

Test 3

Cambridge B2 First Use of English

Part 1

For questions 1–8, read the text below and decide which answer best fits each gap. In the separate answer sheet, mark the appropriate answer (A, B, C or D).

Teenage depression

Depression among teenagers has become a serious concern in today's society. That's why it's crucial not to **(1)**_____ the problem by simply blaming it on typical teenage changes in mood. All of us can feel **(2)**_____ the weather from time to time, but ongoing feelings of sadness or a lack of interest in activities once enjoyed could be signs of something more serious.

You might wonder why depression is having **(3)**_____ on so many young people's lives.

A lot of teens blame schools for this problem. They often feel **(4)**_____ by the school workload and expectations of both parents and teachers. Meeting so many demands that they can't **(5)**_____ with may lead to feeling like a failure.

Another **(6)**_____ to consider is the influence of social media. Teenagers may feel inferior when comparing themselves to social media influencers.

There's no denying the fact that family issues also play a significant role in teenage depression. Teens **(7)**_____ to feel misunderstood, unloved and lonely when there are conflicts or a lack of support or affection within the family.

By **(8)**_____ the problem early enough, we can provide the right support to help teenagers overcome depression in order to lead healthy lives.

1	A	ignore	B	prioritise	C	take	D	face
2	A	below	B	down	C	beneath	D	under
3	A	A change	B	a strike	C	an impact	D	A hit
4	A	bored	B	pressured	C	exhausted	D	anxious
5	A	manage	B	handle	C	cope	D	tackle
6	A	factor	B	condition	C	circumstance	D	element
7	A	intend	B	pretend	C	resent	D	tend
8	A	recognising	B	coping	C	instructing	D	realising

Part 2

For questions 9–16, read the text below and decide which word best fits each gap. Use only one word for each gap. In the separate answer sheet, write your answers in capital letters, using one box per letter.

Why learning languages matters

Nowadays being fluent in at least one foreign language is essential, especially in a world that is becoming increasingly 'globalised'.

There are a number of different reasons why you should be able to communicate in other languages **(9)**_____ ease. To begin with, even if it fails **(10)**_____ unlock the door to your dream job, having a second language will definitely widen your career options. In the competitive job market, employers will highly value candidates who stand **(11)**_____ from the crowd due to their knowledge of multiple languages.

Secondly, for those passionate **(12)**_____ travelling and exploring new places, the ability to communicate with locals in their native language can make them feel confident and more prepared. It also allows for more authentic experiences while travelling.

However, there is another compelling argument for language learning that **(13)**_____ beyond professional or travel motivations. Learning a language is a perfect mental exercise for your brain. **(14)**_____ more you put your brain to use, the stronger and bigger it gets. It **(15)**_____ said that people who know other languages are more creative and better problem solvers. They excel **(16)**_____ multitasking and are more adaptable in today's fast-paced world.

Are you ready to start learning today?

Part 3

For questions 17–24, use the stem word on the right to form the correct word that fills each gap. In the separate answer sheet, write your answers in capital letters, using one box per letter.

The pride of Polish tennis

If you had asked a foreigner a few years ago to give you the name of a **(17)**_____ Polish sportsperson, you'd probably have heard the name Robert Lewandowski. However, nowadays, more and more people mention Iga Świątek as a **(18)**_____ star of women's tennis.

SUCCESS

RISE

Despite her young age, her **(19)**_____ are really impressive. In 2020, at the age of 19, she won The French Open singles title, becoming the first Polish player to do so. With her **(20)**_____ skills on the court, she went on to take the world of tennis by storm and in the following years she won yet more titles. One of her greatest **(21)**_____ is her forehand, and her playing style can be described as both aggressive and dynamic.

ACHIEVE

REMARK

STRONG

Iga is also **(22)**_____ involved with many organisations. She is particularly concerned about mental health issues, and that's why she offers **(23)**_____ support to such initiatives. Iga **(24)**_____ admits how important sports psychologists are, as they help athletes prepare mentally for competitions.

ACT

SUBSTANCE
OPEN

Part 4

For questions 25–30, complete the second sentence, using the word given, so that it has a similar meaning to the first sentence. Do not change the word provided and use between two and five words in total. In the separate answer sheet, write your answers in capital letters, using one box per letter.

25 When does the shop open on Saturdays?
   KNOW
   Do you _____ on Saturdays?

26 "I'm sorry, I lied to you," Amanda said.
   APOLOGISED
   Amanda _____ the truth.

27 We had better save money for a rainy day.
   BE
   Money _____ for a rainy day.

28 I'm fed up with the way you treat me badly.
   TREATED
   I'm tired _____ you.

29 I'm sure Elena hasn't finished her project yet.
   HAVE
   Elena _____ her project already.

30 New York isn't as far from Boston as it is from Los Angeles.
   THAN
   New York is _____ Boston.

Answer sheet: Cambridge B2 First
Use of English

Test No. ☐

Mark out of 36 ☐

Name _____   **Date** _____

Part 1: Multiple choice   8 marks

Mark the appropriate answer (A, B, C or D).

| 0 | A | **B** | C | D |

1	A	B	C	D		5	A	B	C	D
2	A	B	C	D		6	A	B	C	D
3	A	B	C	D		7	A	B	C	D
4	A	B	C	D		8	A	B	C	D

Part 2: Open cloze   8 marks

Write your answers in capital letters, using one box per letter.

| 0 | B | E | C | A | U | S | E | | | |

9 ☐☐☐☐☐☐☐☐☐☐
10 ☐☐☐☐☐☐☐☐☐☐
11 ☐☐☐☐☐☐☐☐☐☐
12 ☐☐☐☐☐☐☐☐☐☐
13 ☐☐☐☐☐☐☐☐☐☐
14 ☐☐☐☐☐☐☐☐☐☐
15 ☐☐☐☐☐☐☐☐☐☐
16 ☐☐☐☐☐☐☐☐☐☐

Part 3: Word formation

8 marks

Write your answers in capital letters, using one box per letter.

17.
18.
19.
20.
21.
22.
23.
24.

Part 4: Key word transformation

12 marks

Write your answers in capital letters, using one box per letter.

25.
26.
27.
28.
29.
30.

Cambridge B2 First Use of English

Test 4

Cambridge B2 First Use of English

Part 1

For questions 1–8, read the text below and decide which answer best fits each gap. In the separate answer sheet, mark the appropriate answer (A, B, C or D).

Public transport: To use or not to use?

A lot of people use public transport to commute to work or school on a regular **(1)**_____, and they often express dissatisfaction with it.

First of all, if they live in a small village, there may be a problem with the **(2)**_____ public transport networks available. Buses or trains simply don't **(3)**_____ frequently enough. There are so few of them during the day that it is necessary to **(4)**_____ one's time carefully to avoid being late for work or missing the last bus home.

Secondly, some people decide not to give it a **(5)**_____ because they believe it usually takes longer to get somewhere using public transport. Buses are often delayed, and after getting off at the bus stop people often have to walk a kilometre or more to their destination.

Another reason is overcrowding. Not being able to secure **(6)**_____, and being packed among other passengers can make journeys uncomfortable. Some commuters also claim that public transport **(7)**_____ are relatively high when considering the quality of the transport on offer.

However, despite its disadvantages, public transport can actually enhance people's happiness. It eliminates the stress associated with driving, the **(8)**_____ to find parking space as well as the expense of buying petrol

So, maybe next time it's worth considering this option.

1	A	ground	B	routine	C	basis	D	occasion
2	A	peculiar	B	limited	C	mere	D	uncommon
3	A	run	B	take	C	drive	D	go
4	A	supervise	B	observe	C	monitor	D	regulate
5	A	start	B	turn	C	trial	D	go
6	A	seating	B	position	C	place	D	occupation
7	A	expenses	B	fares	C	tariffs	D	charges
8	A	necessity	B	obligation	C	demand	D	duty

Part 2

For questions 9–16, read the text below and decide which word best fits each gap. Use only one word for each gap. In the separate answer sheet, write your answers in capital letters, using one box per letter.

The 2023 Turkey-Syria Earthquake

An earthquake is **(9)**_____ of the most terrible natural disasters. It can result **(10)**_____ the ground shaking and falling rocks or earth. The extent of destruction caused **(11)**_____ an earthquake depends on the local geology, the intensity of the earthquake and its duration.

The earthquake that occurred in Turkey and Syria in February 2023 had a 7.8 magnitude and lasted for 85 seconds. It was so strong that it was felt as **(12)**_____ away as Egypt, Lebanon, Cyprus and Iraq, and caused many minor earthquakes in the following months. Tragically, more than 50,000 people lost their lives and it was described as the worst earthquake the region **(13)**_____ seen in 20 years. Many buildings were completely destroyed while **(14)**_____ suffered serious damage, leaving several million people homeless. In fact, only a few buildings were left untouched.

After a year, many of the affected areas were still in ruins, and people were living in **(15)**_____ of another earthquake striking the area. To **(16)**_____ matters worse, even now people living there do not have much hope for their future.

Cambridge B2 First Use of English

Part 3

For questions 17–24, use the stem word on the right to form the correct word that fills each gap. In the separate answer sheet, write your answers in capital letters, using one box per letter.

What can make us happy at work?

As we spend most of our time at work, the feeling of happiness in the workplace plays an important role in our lives. But what factors contribute to making our work (17)_____? **ENJOY**

It may be (18)_____, but contrary to popular belief **EXPECT**
money is not the sole deciding factor. Instead, there are other, more important aspects. Being very well-paid certainly is satisfying, but (19)_____ for our work also counts. **APPRECIATE**
Workers should know that their hard work is valued and recognised. It will make them more committed and (20)_____ about their tasks. **ENTHUSIASM**

Another important factor is a good relationship with our colleagues. People who get on well with their co-workers are more likely to perform well and are more (21)_____ **EFFECT**
team players.

For those who seek a healthy work-life balance, having (22)_____ in their work schedule is extremely **FLEXIBLE**
important. It allows them to concentrate on completing tasks rather than working a fixed number of hours.

Most importantly, research shows that making an employee feel happy at work is also (23)_____ for the employer. **BENEFIT**
A satisfied worker is definitely much more (24)_____ **PRODUCE**
than their unhappy colleague. Isn't this what should concern an employer the most?

Part 4

For questions 25–30, complete the second sentence, using the word given, so that it has a similar meaning to the first sentence. Do not change the word provided and use between two and five words in total. In the separate answer sheet, write your answers in capital letters, using one box per letter.

25 Students were bored with the lesson.

   NOT

   Students _____ interesting.

26 Joseph, do you think you could climb Mount Everest?

   CAPABLE

   Joseph, _____ Mount Everest?

27 You use the key to open the door.

   FOR

   The key _____ the door.

28 I prefer reading books to watching films.

   THAN

   I'd _____ watch films.

29 There is no way we will be on time for the film.

   WILL

   The film _____ by the time we get to the cinema.

30 It doesn't seem sensible to buy another dress that you are not going to wear.

   POINT

   There _____ another dress that you are not going to wear.

Answer sheet: Cambridge B2 First
Use of English

Test No. ☐

Mark out of 36 ☐

Name _____ Date _____

Part 1: Multiple choice   8 marks

Mark the appropriate answer (A, B, C or D).

| 0 | A **B** C D |

1	A B C D		5	A B C D
2	A B C D		6	A B C D
3	A B C D		7	A B C D
4	A B C D		8	A B C D

Part 2: Open cloze   8 marks

Write your answers in capital letters, using one box per letter.

| 0 | B | E | C | A | U | S | E | | | |

9.
10.
11.
12.
13.
14.
15.
16.

Part 3: Word formation

8 marks

Write your answers in capital letters, using one box per letter.

17.
18.
19.
20.
21.
22.
23.
24.

Part 4: Key word transformation

12 marks

Write your answers in capital letters, using one box per letter.

25.
26.
27.
28.
29.
30.

Cambridge
B2 First
Use of English

Test 5

Cambridge B2 First Use of English

Part 1

For questions 1–8, read the text below and decide which answer best fits each gap. In the separate answer sheet, mark the appropriate answer (A, B, C or D).

Dealing with bad neighbours

Most of us will have heard countless stories about 'bad neighbours'. There is no **(1)**_____ that having an annoying neighbour can be a real nuisance. However, what you must realise is that you do not have to **(2)**_____ such unacceptable behaviour.

Here are some suggestions for how to handle a person who **(3)**_____ you crazy:

First of all, introduce yourself at the first opportunity. It will be much harder for a neighbour to cause you trouble if you are friendly. **(4)**_____ talk to them. It is possible that they are not aware of the fact that they are disturbing anyone. For example, a neighbour who has difficulty hearing well and so turns the TV up full **(5)**_____ may not realise that you can hear it in your home as well.

If these suggestions don't work, you could consider asking someone for professional help. Check **(6)**_____ there are such services on offer in your area. They aim to help two sides **(7)**_____ an agreement.

Who knows, maybe one day, with the right approach, a difficult neighbour will transform **(8)**_____ your good friend.

1	A	explanation	B	possibility	C	doubt	D	evidence
2	A	bear	B	cope	C	deal	D	suffer
3	A	makes	B	causes	C	puts	D	drives
4	A	Soon	B	Eventually	C	Then	D	Quickly
5	A	sound	B	blast	C	power	D	pitch
6	A	when	B	if	C	whereas	D	whilst
7	A	reach	B	come	C	gain	D	acquire
8	A	out	B	away	C	over	D	into

Part 2

For questions 9–16, read the text below and decide which word best fits each gap. Use only one word for each gap. In the separate answer sheet, write your answers in capital letters, using one box per letter.

Unexpected problems at the airport

Even the most seasoned tourist faces some unexpected problems at the airport from time to time. **(9)**_____ their best efforts, complications can occur, requiring travellers to adjust to unforeseen circumstances. Here are some tips on how to prepare yourself in advance to **(10)**_____ some of them.

Check whether you have a valid passport. Do this **(11)**_____ advance so that you have time to renew it if necessary. Some countries require passports to be valid for six months beyond your entry date. And, of course, remember to bring it **(12)**_____ you on your trip!

Keep track of time. **(13)**_____ late is not an option. Arrive at the airport early to allow plenty of time for checking in, going through security and reaching the gate before it closes.

Your name, phone number and address should **(14)**_____ attached to your suitcase in case it gets lost. By doing this, the officials will be able to get in touch with you if they find your luggage. By the time you realise it has been lost, they may **(15)**_____ already contacted you about its recovery.

Follow any safety instructions or guidelines given by airport staff. If you are not sure about something, don't be afraid to ask them for assistance. Their role is **(16)**_____ help you and ensure that you have a safe and uncomplicated journey.

Part 3

For questions 17–24, use the stem word on the right to form the correct word that fills each gap. In the separate answer sheet, write your answers in capital letters, using one box per letter.

The phenomenon of social media

In the past, before the rise of social media, young people didn't have the same opportunities to become a celebrity as they do now. Today, social media plays a **(17)**_____ role in shaping youth culture. A lot of young people dream about becoming **(18)**_____. They want to make themselves a so-called '**(19)**_____ name', and they believe that they can do this through their online activity.

SIGNIFY
FAME
HOUSE

This phenomenon has both pros and cons. On one hand, a young person can express their **(20)**_____ and show their talents or values by using social networking sites. Because of their **(21)**_____ on social media, they could have a greater opportunity to develop their artistic, social or media careers.

IDENTIFY
PRESENT

On the other hand, the sudden **(22)**_____ that young people can achieve may have a negative influence on their well-being. What's more, to achieve social media success requires spending a vast amount of time online, which can affect their private life.

POPULAR

Social media is a **(23)**_____ innovation, but it is important to know how to maintain a healthy balance between online and offline life, and to remember the values that matter the most. It is vital to raise young people's **(24)**_____ of both the benefits and the risks associated with their use of social media.

BENEFIT

AWARE

Part 4

For questions 25–30, complete the second sentence, using the word given, so that it has a similar meaning to the first sentence. Do not change the word provided and use between two and five words in total. In the separate answer sheet, write your answers in capital letters, using one box per letter.

25 I was surprised to learn that Elaine can't cook and Suzanna can't cook either.
    NOR
    I was surprised to learn that _____ cook.

26 Stefan is not willing to go to the party.
    FEEL
    Stefan _____ to the party.

27 I wish I hadn't lied to her.
    TOLD
    I wish _____ the truth.

28 "Did you buy Karl a present?" Helena asked me.
    WHETHER
    Helena asked _____ Karl a present.

29 I believe that both Ivan and Tomas enjoy climbing.
    SO
    Ivan enjoys climbing and _____, I believe.

30 Did Patricia sing the song?
    SANG
    Was _____ the song?

Answer sheet: Cambridge B2 First Use of English

Test No. ☐

Mark out of 36 ☐

Name _____ **Date** _____

Part 1: Multiple choice   8 marks

Mark the appropriate answer (A, B, C or D).

| 0 | A | **B** | C | D |

1	A B C D		5	A B C D
2	A B C D		6	A B C D
3	A B C D		7	A B C D
4	A B C D		8	A B C D

Part 2: Open cloze   8 marks

Write your answers in capital letters, using one box per letter.

| 0 | B | E | C | A | U | S | E | | | |

9										
10										
11										
12										
13										
14										
15										
16										

Part 3: Word formation

8 marks

Write your answers in capital letters, using one box per letter.

17										
18										
19										
20										
21										
22										
23										
24										

Part 4: Key word transformation

12 marks

Write your answers in capital letters, using one box per letter.

25																
26																
27																
28																
29																
30																

Answers

Cambridge B2 Use of English

Test 1

Part 1: Multiple choice							
1	C	for		5	D	admire
2	A	either		6	C	spend
3	B	for instance		7	A	head
4	B	get		8	C	stick

Part 2: Open cloze				
9	by		13	be
10	to		14	among/amongst
11	also		15	take
12	and/or/which		16	up

Part 3: Word formation				
17	unexpected		21	strength
18	adequately		22	unlikely
19	improvement		23	extraordinary
20	actions		24	unavoidable

Part 4: Key word transformation	
25	was called/put off – had/needed to be called/put off
26	have not/haven't seen Peter for/in
27	In spite of his illness/being ill/feeling ill
28	am having my flat redecorated
29	If I were you
30	needn't/need not have bought/did not need to buy

Test 2

Part 1: Multiple choice

1	D	staying	5	A	hit
2	A	Nevertheless	6	D	for
3	C	bear	7	A	regardless
4	B	in	8	B	but

Part 2: Open cloze

9	for	13	to
10	need/may/might	14	number/amount/range
11	making	15	on
12	long	16	which

Part 3: Word formation

17	consideration	21	substantial
18	exaggeration	22	Additionally
19	remarkable	23	physical
20	revolutionary	24	improvement

Part 4: Key word transformation

25	I had difficulty hearing
26	wish (that) you would/you'd stop
27	may not have broken
28	will/'ll have watched
29	accused Mark of lying/having lied
30	promised not to be/promised he wouldn't be

Cambridge B2 Use of English

Test 3

Part 1: Multiple choice						
1	A	ignore	5	C	cope
2	D	under	6	B	factor
3	C	impact	7	D	tend
4	B	pressured	8	A	recognising

Part 2: Open cloze				
9	with	13	goes
10	to	14	The
11	out	15	is
12	about	16	in

Part 3: Word formation				
17	successful	21	strengths
18	rising	22	actively
19	achievements	23	substantial
20	remarkable	24	openly

Part 4: Key word transformation	
25	know when the shop opens
26	apologised for not telling (me/him/her)
27	should be saved/ought to be saved
28	of being treated badly by
29	can't/couldn't have finished
30	further from Los Angeles than

Test 4

Part 1: Multiple choice

1	C	basis	5	D	go
2	B	limited	6	A	seating
3	A	run	7	B	fares
4	C	monitor	8	A	necessity

Part 2: Open cloze

9	one	13	had
10	in	14	others
11	by	15	fear
12	far	16	make

Part 3: Word formation

17	enjoyable	21	effective
18	unexpected	22	flexibility
19	appreciation	23	beneficial
20	enthusiastic	24	productive

Part 4: Key word transformation

25	did not/didn't find the lesson
26	are you capable of climbing
27	is (used) for opening
28	rather read books than
29	will have begun/started
30	is/'s no point (in) buying

Cambridge B2 Use of English

Test 5

Part 1: Multiple choice						
1	C	doubt		5	B	blast
2	A	bear		6	B	if
3	D	drives		7	A	reach
4	C	Then		8	D	into

Part 2: Open cloze			
9	Despite	13	Being
10	avoid	14	be
11	in	15	have
12	with	16	to

Part 3: Word formation			
17	significant	21	presence
18	famous	22	popularity
19	household	23	beneficial
20	identity	24	awareness

Part 4: Key word transformation	
25	neither Elaine nor Suzanna can
26	does not/doesn't feel like/up to going
27	I had told her
28	(me) whether I had bought
29	so does Tomas
30	it Patricia who sang

Bonus material

Reading First: Eight more practice tests for the Cambridge B2 First
Published: 2023
ISBN: 9781915654069
Book 2: 8 Reading practice tests (Parts 5–7) with answer keys, write-in answer sheets and a marking scheme

 View this resource and our other Cambridge B2 First materials on **Amazon**.

 Purchase direct as a printed book or downloadable PDF from our **website**.

Use of English: Another ten practice tests for the Cambridge B2 First
Published: 2023
ISBN: 9781915654052
Book 3. 10 Use of English practice tests (Parts 1–4) with answer keys, answer sheets and a marking scheme

 View this resource and our other Cambridge B2 First materials on **Amazon**.

 Purchase direct as a printed book or downloadable PDF from our **website**.

Cambridge B2 First Reading

Test 1

Cambridge B2 First Reading

Part 5

You are going to read an extract from a blog in which a man named Hartmann Gumason talks about the World's Strongest Man competition. For questions 31–36, read the text below and decide which answer fits best according to the text. In the separate answer sheet, mark the appropriate answer (A, B, C or D).

Preparing for the World's Strongest Man competition is a demanding process, but it's also a rewarding one. First of all, I have to consume a lot of calories to fuel my training. I usually eat around 8,000 to 10,000 calories per day, relying on a diet that's high in protein-rich foods like lean meat, fish and eggs, carbohydrates and healthy fats. I also have to eat frequently throughout the day to reach my calorie goal, so I'm constantly snacking on things like nuts and berries in between multiple large meals.

Secondly, building up almost super-human strength requires intense weightlifting and functional fitness exercises. I train for several hours a day, six days a week, and I focus on exercises that will help me perform well in the competition. This includes lifting heavy weights.

It's important to take care of your body while training, and I make sure to warm up properly before each workout, stretch regularly and take it easy on the days when I'm feeling particularly tired or sore. At the same time, it's essential to push yourself to reach your goals.

Preparation for the World's Strongest Man competition requires a great deal of dedication, and I've had to give up some of my social life and devote all of my time and energy to training. It can also be difficult to maintain relationships with friends who don't understand the time and dedication required to compete at this level. But I'm lucky, I have a network of people who understand and support my goals.

Training also costs a fortune. There are gym memberships, supplements, and equipment, as well as the high cost of travel from Iceland to many different competition venues and expensive lodging for the competition. I mean, it's great to see the world while I'm competing, but it does come at a price early on, I cut down a lot so I wouldn't miss out. But I have made up my mind to give 100 percent to make it to the competition, and I believe it will be worth it.

Of course, I couldn't do any of this without the support of my sponsors. It's vital to have a solid brand and a strong and constant social media presence. This allows you to showcase your achievements, training and personality to a wider audience, and, for some competitors, attract potential sponsors. I make sure to consistently perform at my best and maintain a positive image, both on and off the competition stage, for the reputation of the sponsors. At the same time, I believe in building and maintaining strong relationships with my sponsors, who I mostly meet at competitions. I keep in touch with them, as, to me, it's crucial to provide regular updates on my training and competition progress, and show my appreciation for their support. By doing this, I am able to keep their interest and ensure that the partnership benefits us both.

If you're curious about being a strongman or preparing for the competition, my advice would be to make up your mind that you're going to commit to the tough training schedule, do your research on the challenges your body will face and consider the costs. You could even start putting some money aside for training or when a competition comes up. Don't forget to share your experiences with your family and friends, and find a supportive community of competitors.

It's not an easy path, but it's incredibly satisfying and the sense of achievement you feel when you step on the competition stage is unmatched. So, go for it, and give it your all!

Test 1

31 What does Hartmann suggest about his meals?

   A He tends to stick to strict mealtimes.
   B He has to regularly calculate his calorie intake.
   C He has to eat food he doesn't enjoy.
   D He eats a varied diet to meet his calorie target.

32 What point about his training does he make in paragraph three?

   A That working hard and resting are equally important.
   B That training hard can make your body ache.
   C That warming up and stretching must be done simultaneously.
   D That resting can only happen when not preparing for a competition.

33 What does Hartmann say about his relationships?

   A He prefers training to socialising with friends and family.
   B He can't have friends because of the demands of his training.
   C He thinks that his family struggles to understand the effort his training requires.
   D He has a group of people who appreciate his commitment to training.

34 What does Hartmann say about the financial aspects of his lifestyle?

   A the travel opportunities are what make the costs worth it.
   B he gave up things in the past to help him in the future.
   C the accommodation is often the most expensive part.
   D he nearly gave up because of rising costs.

35 How does Hartmann feel about his sponsors?

   A His sponsors increases the amount of pressure.
   B He and his sponsors both see the advantages in their relationship.
   C His sponsors require him to provide frequent updates on his training.
   D He can only gain good sponsors and deals through social media.

36 Hartmann's main point in the final paragraph about training and competing is that

   A it is important to socialise with people with similar interests.
   B you have to be physically and mentally strong.
   C it is worth doing despite the sacrifices you have to make.
   D you need to have enough money before you start competing.

Cambridge B2 First Reading

Part 6

You are going to read an extract from an article in which a careers adviser gives advice on choosing a university. Six sentences have been removed. For questions 37–42, read the text below and, in the separate answer sheet, choose from options A–G the sentence that fits each gap. There is one extra sentence that you do not need to use.

Choosing a university

A careers adviser suggests how to choose a university

As a careers adviser, I'm often asked by students about the best way to look for a suitable university course when finishing school. It's a critical decision, and one that can have a significant impact on a person's future, so it's essential to approach the process with careful consideration.

Firstly, I always advise students to look into a variety of courses that interest them but also not to stick to things they know. **37**☐ You might be surprised to find that something that you never thought you'd be interested in could turn out to be a great option for you.

There are subjects available that you might never even have heard of, so it's important to look beyond the school curriculum. **38**☐ You can do anything, and not just the typical subjects you learn at school.

Once you have a list of potential courses, it's time to weigh up the pros and cons of each one. Consider the course content, the reputation of the university, the location and the potential job prospects after graduation. Make a list of these key factors and other things that are most important to you, and use it to evaluate each course on your list.

39☐ Unless you have a million pounds in the bank, you'll need to consider the cost of tuition, accommodation and other living expenses. How are you going to get home in the holidays? How much is rent in the student halls or rented houses? Think about how you'll pay for everything and what support might be available to you, such as scholarships or student loans. The university will often have a list of potential sources of funding.

As soon as you've reduced your list to a handful of potential courses, it's time to start doing your research. Attend university open days and information sessions, talk to current students and read up on the course content and requirements. **40**☐ The more you know about each course, the institution and the fees, the easier it will be to make an informed decision.

When it comes to making the final decision, it's essential to trust your instincts. If a course feels like a good choice for you, and you can picture yourself enjoying the subject matter and succeeding in the university environment, it's likely that you've made the right choice. **41**☐ You need to make sure you're making the right decision, because it's a big financial commitment.

Finally, don't be afraid to seek guidance and support from others. Talk to your teachers, parents and careers advisers about your options, and get their advice on how to approach the decision-making process. It can be helpful to get an outside perspective and to discuss ideas with someone who has experience in this area.

Overall, looking for a suitable university course when finishing school is a complex process that requires careful consideration and research. **42**☐ By following these steps, you'll be well on your way to finding the perfect course for you and taking the next step towards a bright and fulfilling future.

Test 1

A It's important to look into a range of courses, think about the positives and negatives of each one, consider the practicalities and do your research.

B On the other hand, you may decide that you want to stick to something you already know, such as history, maths, or a foreign language.

C What about comedy, the science of baking, or oil and gas management, for instance?

D You could also search YouTube, for example, as it's usually possible to find 'day in the life' videos by students at the university you're considering.

E It's also crucial to consider the financial practicalities of each course.

F That way, they can keep an open mind and explore a range of subjects to see what might be a good fit.

G However, if you have any doubts, it's important to listen to those too.

Cambridge B2 First Reading

Part 7

You are going to read a newspaper article about a newspaper article about learning a language. Six sentences have been removed. For questions 43–52, read the text below and, in the separate answer sheet, choose the correct paragraph (A–D).

Learning a language

Four people describe how they feel about learning foreign languages

A Steve: I've always been fascinated by foreign languages, and I'm finally learning one on my own! It's challenging, but I'm optimistic that I can do it, and I much prefer it to taking lessons. I've found that the best approach is to build up my skills slowly, starting with the basics and gradually adding more complex concepts. To vary things, I like to listen to music and watch movies in the language that I'm learning. This not only helps me practise my listening skills but also exposes me to new vocabulary, and I get to learn about the culture as well. When I find all the learning too much, I take a quick break to recharge, and usually do something different each time. I find walking outside or going to the gym helps me get back my focus and enthusiasm. To me, learning a new language is a great way to expand your horizons and open up new possibilities for work.

B Borja: Taking up a foreign language has been a real struggle for me. I find it hard to note down everything the teacher says, and I'm constantly worried about getting things wrong when I hand in my essays and written assignments. It's difficult to make sense of the grammar rules and vocabulary, and I often feel bored to tears during class. Equally, I find it hard to stay motivated when I feel like I'm not making progress. While some people seem to pick up languages easily, I'm finding it very challenging. I don't think it's something that comes naturally to me. I wish I could appreciate the process more, but it feels like hard work. Despite the difficulties, I know that knowing a foreign language can be an incredibly helpful thing for when I go abroad, and I'm determined to push through.

C Pallavi: Learning a foreign language has always been a piece of cake for me because I'm great with technology! If you're struggling to pick up a new language, I have some tips that might help from when I was studying and taking lessons. First, look through online resources and apps that can make learning fun and interactive and make notes if you like doing so. Second, set aside specific time each day to practise, and use the same tools and techniques each time to reinforce your learning. Similarly, absorbing yourself in the language by listening to music, watching movies and speaking with native speakers. Finally, don't be afraid to make mistakes! The more you practise, the better you'll get. Practise every day and keep at it, and before you know it you'll be a fluent speaker! It took me a while, but I got there eventually!

D Adriana: Learning a new language is something I have always wanted to take up, so I decided to sign up for a course through work. It's been a great way to get into the language and learn more about the culture. To be honest, it's been tricky but also very rewarding. At first, it was challenging to feel confident and keep up with the pace of the group, although I eventually got there. I find that practising regularly and doing activities outside of class helps me to stay on track. So far, I have learned a lot of new vocabulary and grammar, and I am starting to feel more confident when speaking, even though I still make mistakes. Overall, I think that learning a new language is worthwhile, and I am happy that I decided to give it a try. I still have a long way to go before I can consider myself fluent, but I am excited to continue learning.

Test 1

Which person:

states that learning a foreign language can be a useful skill for travelling? | 43 |

finds learning a language to be quite straightforward? | 44 |

thinks that learning with others was initially difficult? | 45 |

mentions that they do not have a natural ability for languages? | 46 |

explains that making errors is part of the learning process? | 47 |

thinks that it's essential to develop a routine when learning? | 48 |

suggests learning a new language creates employment opportunities? | 49 |

believes that they will succeed with their self-study? | 50 |

says that extra work in addition to lessons helps them to focus? | 51 |

mentions how they feel about written work? | 52 |

Cambridge B2 First Use of English

Answer sheet   Test No. ☐

                                                      Mark out of 22 ☐

Name _____   Date _____

Part 5   *6 marks*

Mark the appropriate answer (A, B, C or D).

| 0 | A | B | **C** | D |

31	A	B	C	D		34	A	B	C	D
32	A	B	C	D		35	A	B	C	D
33	A	B	C	D		36	A	B	C	D

Part 6   *6 marks*

Add the appropriate answer (A–G).

| 37 | 38 | 39 |
| 40 | 41 | 42 |

Part 7   *10 marks*

Add the appropriate answer (A, B, C or D).

| 43 | 44 | 45 | 46 | 47 |
| 48 | 49 | 50 | 51 | 52 |

Cambridge B2 First Reading

Test 2

Cambridge B2 First Reading

Part 5

You are going to read an extract from an interview in which Sam Godfrey talks about the Young Musician of the Year competition. For questions 31–36, read the text below and decide which answer fits best according to the text. In the separate answer sheet, mark the appropriate answer (A, B, C or D).

My name is Sam Godfrey and I am currently involved in the Young Musician of the Year competition. I first realised that I might have a chance of winning the competition about a year ago when my music teacher and I spoke at a school music festival, and she suggested that I try out for it in front of judges. I was hesitant to apply at first because I knew the competition would be difficult and that the level of talent was going to be extremely high. However, after looking it up online, I decided to try, and I was happy when I found out that I had been selected to compete. It was a great moment when I read the acceptance email; I still can't believe it.

Competing in the Young Musician of the Year competition has been challenging. Honestly, all the other competitors are so good. Every musician here is talented in their own way, and it can be stressful at times to know how to succeed. I have to do everything I can to stand out, and that includes building my brand both online and offline, which I've just begun doing. On the other hand, it's also incredibly inspiring to be surrounded by so much talent and to learn from my peers.

The preparation is hard, but having a routine of sorts definitely helps. It's been a bit of a struggle though, especially since I've been living out of a suitcase for the past few weeks and travelling here, there and everywhere. But I've found ways to stay focused and maintain my routine, even when things get busy. I make time for practice every day, and I always make sure to eat healthily and get enough rest. Additionally, I surround myself with positive people who inspire me.

Winning the competition would be a dream come true. Of course, that is my goal – to take home the grand prize and be crowned the Young Musician of the Year. It would be an incredible achievement and recognition of all the hard work I've put in. But even if that doesn't happen, I want to walk away from this experience having pushed myself to the limits, pleased with myself and the effort I've put in and having grown as a musician. I want to prove to myself and to others that, with hard work and dedication, anything is possible. Whether I win or not, I'll walk away with admiration for every single person that has taken part in this challenging process.

Line 26　It would also be a way for me to share my music with a wider audience and inspire others to go after their passions. Therefore, I hope to use my win as a springboard to help my career progress. I plan to continue writing and performing my original music, and to work with other musicians and artists in the industry. And I want to give back by sharing my experience and offering support to other young musicians.

Ultimately, my objective is to make a meaningful impact on the music world and to be remembered as a talented artist. Winning the Young Musician of the Year competition would be a huge step in the right direction, and I can't wait to see what the future holds.

Test 2

31 How did the writer become involved with the competition?

- **A** By attending another event.
- **B** By watching something online.
- **C** By asking a friend.
- **D** By asking his teacher to apply for him.

32 In order to be successful in the competition, the writer needs

- **A** to have a strong internet presence.
- **B** to receive an acceptance email.
- **C** to do everything possible to be noticed.
- **D** to read plenty of books.

33 What has made the competition difficult for the writer?

- **A** Not having a schedule.
- **B** Not eating well.
- **C** Not sleeping much.
- **D** Not being based in one place.

34 Winning the competition would make the writer feel

- **A** relieved.
- **B** skilled.
- **C** scared.
- **D** respected.

35 What does 'springboard' mean in line 26?

- **A** A problem to an existing solution.
- **B** Something that requires hope.
- **C** A starting point from which something develops.
- **D** Something that requires a crowd.

36 The writer's main goal is to

- **A** write songs for other musicians and artists.
- **B** influence the music world in a big way.
- **C** create a place to share music.
- **D** become a famous music director.

Cambridge B2 First Reading

Part 6

You are going to read a newspaper article in which the success of the Jurassic World movie series is celebrated. Six sentences have been removed. For questions 37–42, read the text below and, in the separate answer sheet, choose from options A–G the sentence that fits each gap. There is one extra sentence that you do not need to use.

A Roaring Success

The Jurassic World movie franchise has been extremely successful since the first film's release in the early 1990s.

The franchise has come up with six movies, each one more thrilling than the last, and has broken free of the traditional monster-movie mould. It owes much of its success to the original book, *Jurassic Park*, written by Michael Crichton in 1990. The novel follows the story of a group of scientists and investors who create a theme park filled with dinosaurs. 37

The book was a success, but its 1993 cinematic adaptation by Steven Spielberg was iconic.

In the story, the characters try to avoid the dinosaur and escape, but the T-Rex continues to chase them, eventually destroying one of the cars and leaving the characters alone and scared. This scene is famous for the terrifying way in which the T-Rex appears and the impressive special effects that bring the dinosaur to life.

Unsurprisingly, the film was a hit, and it also made a lot of money. 38

The next films that followed were The Lost World: Jurassic Park (1997) and Jurassic Park III (2001), which similarly feature exciting dinosaur battles and chase scenes that keep viewers on the edge of their seats.

However, the films weren't as successful as the first, so the creators went back to the beginning and early ideas. 39 The film featured larger and more terrifying creatures and was filled with action-packed scenes that left audiences shocked. In one key scene, a storm disables the electric fences and allows the dinosaurs to break free. The T-Rex then attacks the cars carrying the main characters, causing chaos and destruction.

The success of the movie prompted the filmmakers to make a follow-up, and in 2018, Jurassic World: Fallen Kingdom arrived in cinemas. 40

The movie was a hit with fans, and it made over a billion dollars worldwide. The latest film, Jurassic World: Dominion, ends with dinosaurs living peacefully alongside real-world animals.

What makes the Jurassic World films stand out from other monster movies is its ability to create creatures that feel real, despite their prehistoric origins. 41

In conclusion, the Jurassic World movie franchise has basically set the standard for modern monster movies. 42 Whether you're a long-term fan of the original Jurassic Park or a newcomer to the franchise, there's something for everyone in the Jurassic World.

Test 2

A Its impact on pop culture will undoubtedly continue to entertain readers and movie lovers for generations to come.

B The filmmakers have used new technology to create creatures that look and move like real dinosaurs, making the movies feel even more fascinating.

C However, this time, the risks were higher – audiences were used to the latest technology so the special effects had to be better than ever before

D The scientific accuracy and attention to detail made it fascinating for both dinosaur enthusiasts and sci-fi fans, making it an instant hit.

E Therefore, it's no surprise that the franchise is so popular.

F Then there were the books, board games, toys and video games, all of which made even more money.

G After a break, the franchise returned with the movie Jurassic World, which ended up being an even bigger hit than the ones before.

Cambridge B2 First Reading

Part 7

You are going to read an article in which four people talk about living on an island. Six sentences have been removed. For questions 43–52, read the text below and, in the separate answer sheet, choose the correct paragraph (A–D).

Island life in Scotland

A Marta: As a young au pair living on the Isle of Island, this small island in Scotland is simply breath-taking. Compared to my hometown, Islay is a relaxing place, surrounded by stunning natural landscapes. I am constantly amazed by the beauty of this island (when it's not pouring down, of course!) and I feel incredibly grateful to have had the opportunity to live here. Living in a foreign country has definitely been a challenge, but I am so glad that I decided to come here and make this huge change in my life. I signed up for the au pair program as a way to experience a different culture and way of life, and I have not been disappointed. I know that I need to leave soon and return to the real world, but this experience has taught me so much about myself. I will always look back on my time on Islay with fondness and appreciation.

B Brian: My wife and I decided to move from the hustle and bustle of life in Glasgow in Scotland to the quiet island of Mull, in the north of the country. We were both feeling stressed, and we knew we needed a change. The demands of the 9–5 were tough, and we needed to find a way to calm down and enjoy life again. However, the move wasn't straightforward. However, the move wasn't straightforward. First of all, we had to cut down on our expenses in order to make this move happen. We knew that we would be paid little compared to our previous salaries, but we were willing to take that chance in order to have a better quality of life. But it was worth it! Life on Mull is much more relaxed, and we have time to appreciate the small things in life and to enjoy the beauty of nature. We have also made some amazing new friends of different ages in the local community.

C Cameron: I have always lived on the Isle of Skye, and could never imagine living anywhere else. Sometimes, people suggest that I should consider moving to a bigger city for more job opportunities and a high salary. But the truth is that I couldn't turn down the natural beauty and calmness that Skye provides. Besides, I have been fortunate enough to have found a job that I enjoy and which I can do from home. Obviously, if circumstances change and my job suddenly requires me to travel then I might have to consider leaving, but Skye will always hold a special place in my heart and I know I would be a regular visitor if I did leave. I love hiking and taking long walks, and the island offers stunning views that I know it would take me far longer to find on the mainland. In addition, the sense of 'family' here is incredibly special. Everyone knows each other, and there is a strong support system that is very rare elsewhere. I am grateful to have grown up on this island.

D Colin: I live on the small island of Iona, but, to be honest, I can't wait to move away. Don't get me wrong, Iona is beautiful place. But there is not a lot to do for youngsters. Believe me: if you've seen one visitor centre, you've seen them all! I'm still young, so I have to wait a few more years yet, but as soon as I'm old enough I'm moving, maybe to a different country! Some people advise against leaving the island, saying that I'll miss the small community and how quiet life is (I definitely won't!). I feel ready for something new. I've been looking for jobs where I can be a small fish in a big pond for a change. I want to experience new things, meet new people and feel as free as a bird.

Test 2

Which person:

says that they are tired of seeing the same thing more than once?	43	
compares where they live to another country?	44	
refers to the wet weather?	45	
believes that they would return to visit if they moved away?	46	
mentions earning less money than before?	47	
suggests that they want something more exciting to happen to them?	48	
says that they used to be worried and anxious?	49	
suggests that they don't have much time left on their island?	50	
states that they want to see the rest of the world?	51	
explains how the community is refreshingly different from most places?	52	

Cambridge B2 First Use of English

Answer sheet   Test No. [ ]

                                                Mark out of 22 [ ]

Name _____   Date _____

Part 5   *6 marks*

Mark the appropriate answer (A, B, C or D).

| 0 | A B **C** D |

31	A B C D		34	A B C D
32	A B C D		35	A B C D
33	A B C D		36	A B C D

Part 6   *6 marks*

Add the appropriate answer (A–G).

| 37 | 38 | 39 |
| 40 | 41 | 42 |

Part 7   *10 marks*

Add the appropriate answer (A, B, C or D).

| 43 | 44 | 45 | 46 | 47 |
| 48 | 49 | 50 | 51 | 52 |

Cambridge B2 First Reading

Test 3

Cambridge B2 First Use of English

Cambridge B2 First Reading

Part 5

You are going to read an extract from a magazine in which a woman discusses her fear of flying. For questions 31–36, read the text below and decide which answer fits best according to the text. In the separate answer sheet, mark the appropriate answer (A, B, C or D).

I've been afraid of flying for as long as I can remember. It's a fear that comes over me every time I've had to fly, and it took me a long time to try to figure out the reasons why. It's not the fear of the plane falling into the ocean, the plane moving side-to-side in bad weather or even a relatively common fear of heights, although these do scare me. It's the fear of being trapped, the fear of being out of control, the fear of something going wrong and not being able to get out.

Over the years, I've read books on the subject, I've listened to relaxation tapes with supposed calming voices and sounds, and I've even taken a course specifically designed for people with aviophobia, which is the specific term for a fear of flying. While it was initially a good starting point to talk to others who share my same fear, and it helped in many ways, unfortunately, none of these methods fully worked for me. My fear of flying had only grown stronger with each passing year.

I realised that I needed to find a different approach, so I decided to explore therapy. The therapist suggested that we use a method called 'exposure therapy', which involves gradually exposing me to the fear of flying in a controlled environment.

Our first session involved talking generally about my childhood and my fear of flying, before identifying the specific things that caused it. We discussed the physical sensations I experienced when I felt anxious, such as sweating and shaking, as well as the negative thoughts that raced through my mind. My therapist helped me to understand that my fear was unreasonable and that, statistically, the chances of something going wrong on a flight were incredibly low.

Line 19   In the following sessions, we started, in small steps, to face the fear. First, we looked at pictures of planes and airports, then we went on to visit an airport and spoke to a pilot, and, finally, we took a short domestic flight. Each step of the way, my therapist talked me through ways to manage my anxiety and taught me techniques for relaxation and mindfulness that I could do at home.

After months of working together, I felt ready to take a more significant step. I booked a long flight to Europe, something that I never thought I would be able to do. The lead-up to the flight was challenging, and I experienced a lot of anxiety, but I was determined to face my fear.

On the day of the flight, I arrived at the airport early, so I had plenty of time to get through security and settle in before the flight. I used techniques I'd been working on for a while – things my therapist had taught me – to manage my anxiety, including deep-breathing and positive self-talk. I also took medication to help me relax.

The flight was long and challenging, but I made it through. I experienced moments of anxiety, but I was proud of myself for facing my fear and not giving up. When I arrived at my destination, I felt a sense of achievement that I had never experienced before.

Now, a few years later, I still experience some anxiety when I fly, but I manage it much better. I've continued to work with my therapist, and we've even taken another flight together. I've also learned to be more aware and present when I travel, focusing on the sights and experiences around me rather than my fear.

Overcoming my fear of flying and going to therapy have been among the most challenging things I've ever done. However, it's also been one of the most rewarding experiences. I've learned that I'm stronger than my fear. I also feel more confident in myself and my abilities. While I may never love flying, I now know that I can face it and come out the other side.

Test 3

31 What does the writer say she's afraid of when flying?

   A being unable to escape if something bad happens
   B the plane crashing into the water
   C the rough air caused by thunderstorms
   D being in a high place

32 In the second paragraph the writer says that

   A she hadn't ever tried to deal with her fear of flying.
   B sharing her fear of flying with others helped her to some extent.
   C her fear of flying got worse when she knew it had an official name.
   D listening to tapes helped her calm her mind and rest.

33 What did the writer's therapist help her to realise in her first sessions?

   A That the fear had started from a specific moment in her past.
   B That her anxiety produced only mental reactions.
   C That data suggested her fear was illogical.
   D That physical responses were harder to control.

34 What was the main focus of the 'following sessions' in line 19?

   A Talking with an airline captain about her fear.
   B Studying images related to her fear.
   C Being gradually exposed to the fear.
   D Learning to be cautious of the fear.

35 What does the writer say about her flight to Europe?

   A She had been practising strategies to help her in this moment.
   B Her medication was more beneficial than other techniques.
   C She experimented with new techniques to help her relax.
   D Her therapist suggested that arriving early would help her feel calm.

36 How does the writer feel about trying to overcome her fear of flying?

   A She believes that she'll probably enjoy flying more in the future.
   B She says that the challenges of therapy almost made her give up.
   C She thinks that the benefits outweigh the difficulties she faced.
   D She believes that she can overcome the other fears in her life.

Cambridge B2 First Reading

Part 6

You are going to read an extract from a newspaper in which a person talks about public transport improvements. Six sentences have been removed. For questions 37–42, read the text below and, in the separate answer sheet, choose from options A–G the sentence that fits each gap. There is one extra sentence that you do not need to use.

Making Public Transport Attractive

How are governments innovating to improve the use of public transport in cities?

Governments around the world are thinking up new ways to encourage their citizens to use public transport as a way to reduce traffic congestion, air pollution and carbon emissions. [37]

In many cities, people still settle for using their cars as their primary mode of transportation, despite the heavy traffic and high costs associated with this. [38] There are many different ways in which they are doing this.

One example of a government actively promoting public transport is the London Congestion Charge, a fee that drivers must pay to enter the city centre during peak hours. It was first introduced in 2003 as a way to reduce traffic congestion and improve air quality in the city. [39] The introduction of the charge was controversial, with many drivers and businesses opposing it. However, it has been successful in reducing traffic congestion and improving air quality, and it has become a model for other cities around the world. The charge has seen several changes over the years, including an increase in the fee and expansion of the charging zone. It remains a key part of London's transportation policy, and its success has helped to form transportation policy in other cities around the world.

Commuters are more likely to switch if they make a trip on public transport and find that it is good value for money, or find out that it operates 24-7, making it easier to get around.

Therefore, many governments are investing heavily in improving their public transport systems. Tokyo has one of the most advanced and efficient public transport systems in the world, and the city continues to build on its success. One of the most significant improvements in recent years was the introduction of the Tokyo Skytree, a new high-speed train that can take commuters from central Tokyo to the Skytree Tower in just a few minutes. The city also introduced a new mobile app called Navitime that provides real-time information on train schedules and delays, making it easier for commuters to plan their journeys. [40] These improvements have made Tokyo's public transport system even more efficient and convenient for commuters and tourists alike.

[41] For instance, Paris has one of the most successful bike-sharing schemes in the world. Introduced in 2007, it has since become a model for other cities around the world. The *Vélib'* scheme provides more than 14,000 bicycles at 1,230 stations throughout the city, making it easy for people to rent a bike for short trips. [42]

In conclusion, governments are actively trying to encourage people to use public transport by investing in its systems, discussing the benefits of public transport, and introducing interesting new services and technologies. By making it more convenient and attractive, people will be more likely to choose public transport instead of using their cars. This will result in a cleaner, more efficient and longer-lasting transportation system.

A However, governments are now asking its citizens to avoid using their cars and make a journey on public transport instead.

B In addition, this busy city continued to invest in its subway system, introducing new trains and increasing the frequency of service during peak hours.

C Other governments are also coming up with new ideas and introducing new technologies and services that make public transport more convenient and attractive.

D They are also testing out different strategies to improve public transport, making it more reliable, efficient and convenient for people travelling to and from work.

E Only time will tell if these efforts of governments will change people's minds and encourage them to choose greener, more sustainable public transport options.

F At the time, this famous city was one of the most crowded in Europe, with long traffic delays and high levels of air pollution.

G Overall, this project has been a great success for the city and has helped to promote a culture of cycling.

Cambridge B2 First Reading

Part 7

You are going to read a newspaper article about growing old gracefully. Six sentences have been removed. For questions 43–52, read the text below and, in the separate answer sheet, choose the correct paragraph (A–D).

Growing old: The importance of health and well-being

A **Ernest:** Keep active! I have always done some form of physical exercise, and I cannot stress enough the importance of keeping active. Even now, as an armchair sportsman, I still try to keep active as much as possible. One of the best ways to keep active is to make the most of the physical activities that you enjoy. If you love to dance, join in with a local dance class or sing along with a choir. If you enjoy playing games, find a game that involves moving your body. As well as being a great form of exercise, being active can also help you to stay socially connected and improve your mental health. For me, I make an effort to swim twice a week. Swimming is easy on the joints, and it gets the blood moving. It is never too late to start a new activity, and finding something that you enjoy can be the key to staying active and healthy in your later years.

B **Mary:** One of the most important lessons I have learned is that we should focus on the things that make us feel good, both physically and mentally. For me, starting yoga again in my sixties was amazing, and I have found that regular exercise and stretching have helped me to maintain my flexibility and ability to move. I still go to a class every week. However, it's not just physical health that is important as we age. Mental health is just as crucial, and I have found that practising mindfulness is an excellent way to keep my mind sharp and focused. It helps me to reduce stress and anxiety and improve my overall sense of well-being. It has also taught me that if something brings negativity into your life, be it a relationship, a job, or a habit, it's important to cut it out and focus on the things that bring you joy and happiness.

C **Pepe:** One of my favourite sayings is 'A little of what you want does you good', and I believe that this applies to life as well. We don't have to give up everything that we enjoy as we get older, but we do need to learn to take things at a more relaxed pace. It's all too easy to get caught up in the rush of everyday life, but taking the time to slow down and live through each moment can make a big difference to our overall sense of well-being. I have always been incredibly grateful for the simple pleasures in life, such as spending time with my three young grandchildren, reading a good book or simply enjoying a cup of tea. Although it's true that our bodies and minds may not be as strong as they once were, we can still find joy. For me, one of the best things I did was restarting the piano lessons I had given up when I was 14. It's not been easy, but with the help of the many tutorials on the internet, I'm now confident enough to play in front of friends.

D **Margaret:** I find that a good laugh helps me to cheer up and feel younger even if I have a few aches and pains. For that reason, I make it part of my routine to go to my social club at least once a week. I love meeting old friends, making new ones and having a good laugh over a cup of tea. I like to join in with a board game as well. Sometimes I amaze people with the long words I come out with! I also do word searches, and I tackle the crossword every morning in the newspaper – just the simple one, I don't have time for the long one. Due to my love of word games, I started to play puzzles on my phone last year. This has brought me closer to my daughter in Australia as we exchange our scores every day. I love that.

Test 3

Which person:

explains that some forms of meditation are useful for exercising your brain?	43
mentions that growing older doesn't mean you have to stop doing things that make you happy?	44
says that staying sociable lifts your mood even if you're not feeling your best?	45
says that activities keep you physically and mentally healthy and also help you maintain relationships?	46
suggests that you should try to live in the moment every once in a while?	47
thinks both mental and physical health need to be treated equally?	48
likes to play games to stay connected to friends and family?	49
believes that people can enjoy life by appreciating small moments of joy?	50
states that it's possible and beneficial to find new hobbies later in life?	51
thinks that getting rid of pessimistic influences can be necessary at times?	52

Cambridge B2 First Use of English

Answer sheet   Test No. ☐

                                                                             Mark out of 22 ☐

Name _____   Date _____

Part 5   *6 marks*

Mark the appropriate answer (A, B, C or D).

| 0 | A ☐ | B ☐ | C ■ | D ☐ |

31	A ☐	B ☐	C ☐	D ☐		34	A ☐	B ☐	C ☐	D ☐
32	A ☐	B ☐	C ☐	D ☐		35	A ☐	B ☐	C ☐	D ☐
33	A ☐	B ☐	C ☐	D ☐		36	A ☐	B ☐	C ☐	D ☐

Part 6   *6 marks*

Add the appropriate answer (A–G).

| 37 | 38 | 39 |
| 40 | 41 | 42 |

Part 7   *10 marks*

Add the appropriate answer (A, B, C or D).

| 43 | 44 | 45 | 46 | 47 |
| 48 | 49 | 50 | 51 | 52 |

Cambridge B2 First Use of English

Test 1

Cambridge B2 First Use of English

Part 1

For questions 1–8, read the text below and decide which answer best fits each gap. In the separate answer sheet, mark the appropriate answer (A, B, C or D).

Getting the right amount of sleep

Do you ever wake up feeling tired and unrested, **(1)**_____, spending hours in bed? Unfortunately, many people struggle with getting the right amount of sleep, which leads to decreased productivity, mood swings and a host of other health problems.

Getting the right amount of sleep goes hand in hand with a happier and healthier life. Therefore, it's crucial to make the **(2)**_____ of your time in bed. Establish a bedtime **(3)**_____, such as reading or meditating, and create a comfortable sleep environment, including a good mattress and black-out curtains.

Catching up on **(4)**_____ sleep on the weekends can also be helpful, but it's best to **(5)**_____ oversleeping. Getting too much sleep can **(6)**_____ your sleep patterns, making it harder to fall asleep at night and leaving you feeling groggy during the day.

Is it possible to wake up every morning feeling **(7)**_____ and ready to take on the day? The answer is yes! A good night's sleep can make you look like a million dollars, improve your mood and energy **(8)**_____, and better equip you to handle stress.

1	A	despite	B	although	C	for	D	however
2	A	greatest	B	most	C	easiest	D	majority
3	A	procedure	B	schedule	C	hobby	D	routine
4	A	forgotten	B	heavy	C	lost	D	missing
5	A	discontinue	B	escape	C	avoid	D	ignore
6	A	prevent	B	disrupt	C	remove	D	break
7	A	relieved	B	revised	C	reorganised	D	refreshed
8	A	levels	B	feelings	C	zones	D	measures

Test 1

Part 2

For questions 9–16, read the text below and decide which word best fits each gap. Use only one word for each gap. In the separate answer sheet, write your answers in capital letters, using one box per letter.

Cloning

Cloning is the process **(9)**_____ producing genetically identical copies of an organism, tissue or cell. In short, cloning consists of three main steps: obtaining genetic material, growing it in a lab and finally transferring it into a host organism.

Although cloning may seem like science fiction, its origins date back to the early 1900s **(10)**_____ scientists first started experimenting with plant cells. **(11)**_____ it wasn't until 1996 that the world was introduced to the first mammal clone, Dolly the sheep.

Scientists have already come up **(12)**_____ a way to clone animals, but before we know it cloning could be used to create new organs, tissues and even whole humans.

Think again if you thought cloning was only limited **(13)**_____ animals. Scientists are already counting **(14)**_____ to revolutionise agriculture by producing crops that are resistant to pests, disease and extreme weather conditions.

In conclusion, cloning is a fascinating field **(15)**_____ has only just begun to scratch the surface of its potential. We can only imagine in our wildest dreams what could be just **(16)**_____ the corner.

Cambridge B2 First Use of English

Part 3

For questions 17–24, use the stem word on the right to form the correct word that fills each gap. In the separate answer sheet, write your answers in capital letters, using one box per letter.

Street lights

Street lights have been a crucial part of our cities for many years. They play a vital role in **(17)**_____ safety and security during the night. However, the rise in the use of street lights has led to the phenomenon of light pollution, which is becoming a growing concern.

SURE

(18)_____, street lighting accounts for a significant portion of a city's energy consumption. This is particularly true in developed cities where street lighting is used **(19)**_____. For example, London spends more than £30 million on street lighting in a single year. These costs are **(20)**_____, and cities must find ways to reduce the amount of energy used by street lighting while still maintaining adequate lighting levels. **(21)**_____, there are many ways in which this can be done. For example, replacing old sodium lights with new LEDs that give off a whiter light for improved **(22)**_____ LEDs are longer lasting and less likely to fail than traditional street lights, so **(23)**_____ costs are also expected to be lower.

ADD

EXTEND

SUBSTANCE

FORTUNE

VISIBLE

MAINTAIN

The goal should be to provide safe and secure lighting for our communities while **(24)**_____ its impact on the environment.

MINIMUM

Test 1

Part 4

For questions 25–30, complete the second sentence, using the word given, so that it has a similar meaning to the first sentence. Do not change the word provided and use between two and five words in total. In the separate answer sheet, write your answers in capital letters, using one box per letter.

25 I thought of a cheap solution to our computer problems.
    CAME
    I _____ an inexpensive way to solve our computer problems.

26 If you promise to be careful I'll lend you my car.
    LONG
    I'll lend you my car _____ promise to be careful.

27 We haven't arranged a date for the decorators to come.
    BEEN
    A date _____ for the decorators to come.

28 We are introducing reduced membership fees that should help those on lower incomes.
    INTRODUCTION
    _____ new membership fees should help those that earn less.

29 I can help you with the presentation if you want.
    MIND
    I _____ you with the presentation.

30 "James, do you know what time the meeting starts?" asked Shazia.
    IF
    Shazia asked James _____ what time the meeting would start.

Cambridge B2 First Use of English

Answer sheet: Cambridge B2 First Use of English

Test No. ☐

Mark out of 36 ☐

Name _____ Date _____

Part 1: Multiple choice   8 marks

Mark the appropriate answer (A, B, C or D).

| 0 | A **B** C D |

1	A B C D		5	A B C D
2	A B C D		6	A B C D
3	A B C D		7	A B C D
4	A B C D		8	A B C D

Part 2: Open cloze   8 marks

Write your answers in capital letters, using one box per letter.

| 0 | B | E | C | A | U | S | E | | | |

| 9 |
| 10 |
| 11 |
| 12 |
| 13 |
| 14 |
| 15 |
| 16 |

Part 3: Word formation

8 marks

Write your answers in capital letters, using one box per letter.

17.
18.
19.
20.
21.
22.
23.
24.

Part 4: Key word transformation

12 marks

Write your answers in capital letters, using one box per letter.

25.
26.
27.
28.
29.
30.

Cambridge B2 First Use of English

Test 2

Cambridge B2 First Use of English

Part 1

For questions 1–8, read the text below and decide which answer best fits each gap. In the separate answer sheet, mark the appropriate answer (A, B, C or D).

**Wednesday Addams:
The Dark and Quirky Queen of Cool**

Wednesday Addams is the ultimate cool girl. She's the gothic, macabre and quirky daughter of Gomez and Morticia Addams from the Addams Family cartoon and movies and has recently been played by Jenna Ortega in a Netflix series.

Due to her gothic style and dark **(1)**_____ of humour, Wednesday has been winning over teens and young adults for generations. Wednesday's fearlessness is something that many teens today can admire. Her independence and willingness to **(2)**_____ authority make her a relatable and inspiring figure.

Even though Wednesday may come **(3)**_____ as a mischievous troublemaker, she has a strong moral compass and always stands up for what she believes in. This is a quality that is all too **(4)**_____ in today's world, and it's what makes Wednesday such a unique and beloved character.

Wednesday Addams is the epitome of cool. She **(5)**_____ independence, non-conformity and the importance of loyalty to your family. Her dark and quirky personality makes her **(6)**_____ out from the rest and has earned her a place in the **(7)**_____ of fans everywhere. So, if you're looking for inspiration and a **(8)**_____ that it's okay to be different, look no further than Wednesday Addams.

1	A	type	B	quality	C	sense	D	kind
2	A	argue	B	support	C	challenge	D	bother
3	A	across	B	up	C	on	D	with
4	A	odd	B	rare	C	few	D	ordinary
5	A	reflects	B	acts	C	displays	D	represents
6	A	look	B	sit	C	stand	D	put
7	A	hearts	B	eyes	C	brains	D	stomachs
8	A	reminder	B	remember	C	suggestion	D	mention

Test 2

Part 2

For questions 9–16, read the text below and decide which word best fits each gap. Use only one word for each gap. In the separate answer sheet, write your answers in capital letters, using one box per letter.

The mighty sunflower seed

Sunflower seeds are a great source of healthy fats, protein and vitamins, and they make a delicious snack **(9)**_____ roasted. Here you will find out how to roast sunflower seeds and how to incorporate them **(10)**_____ your cooking.

Many store-bought roasted sunflower seeds can be a rip-off, both in terms **(11)**_____ price and quality. Therefore, roasting your own seeds at home is a great **(12)**_____ to cut out the middleman and enjoy delicious, healthy snacks that **(13)**_____ easy on the wallet.

(14)_____ things first, you'll want to dry out your sunflower seeds. Simply spread **(15)**_____ out on a baking sheet and wait for a day or two.

Once your seeds are dry, it's time to start roasting. Place the seeds in a single layer on a baking sheet. Roast for 10-to-12 minutes or **(16)**_____ the seeds are golden brown.

And there you have it! Roasting sunflower seeds is easy, delicious and healthy. Give it a try, and happy roasting!

Cambridge B2 First Use of English

Part 3

For questions 17–24, use the stem word on the right to form the correct word that fills each gap. In the separate answer sheet, write your answers in capital letters, using one box per letter.

Greener alternatives to hand wipes

Hand wipes are a ubiquitous item that have a thousand uses, including cleaning and disinfecting hands on the go. Historically, hand wipes have been around for many years, but they have become **(17)**_____ popular in recent years due to several factors. Firstly, the growing **(18)**_____ of the importance of hand hygiene and secondly, for how **(19)**_____ they are when you're unable to access water. **INCREASE** **AWARE** **CONVENE**

Since the outbreak of the Covid-19 pandemic, the demand for hand wipes has **(20)**_____ and they have become a staple in households and public spaces around the world. **RISE**

It's important to note that hand wipes are not as **(21)**_____ as hand washing with soap and water, but they can be useful in a pinch when soap and water are not available. **EFFECT**

(22)_____, it is important to use environmentally friendly wipes that are biodegradable and free of harsh chemicals. Make sure that you dispose of them in the rubbish bin rather than in your toilet. Aside from the risk to our oceans, waterways and wildlife, water companies spend millions each year **(23)**_____ wet wipes from sewage treatment plants and pumping stations. **ADD** **MOVE**

Alternatively, washable cloth baby-wipes are now **(24)**_____ available and offer a chemical-free alternative to hand wipes. **READY**

Test 2

Part 4

For questions 25–30, complete the second sentence, using the word given, so that it has a similar meaning to the first sentence. Do not change the word provided and use between two and five words in total. In the separate answer sheet, write your answers in capital letters, using one box per letter.

25 Jamie grew up in England with his grandparents.
    RAISED
    Jamie _____ his grandparents in England.

26 "Would it be possible to borrow your car?" asked Ade.
    LEND
    Ade asked _____ her my car.

27 I was told by the doctor that I have to reduce my sugar intake.
    DOWN
    The doctor told me that I need to _____ the amount of sugar I eat.

28 I wish that I hadn't gone out last night.
    REGRET
    I _____ last night.

29 You must wear a safety helmet at all times.
    WORN
    A safety helmet _____ at all times.

30 Otis broke the computer by accident.
    MEAN
    Otis _____ the computer.

Cambridge B2 First Use of English

Answer sheet: Cambridge B2 First
Use of English

Test No. ☐

Mark out of 36 ☐

Name _____   Date _____

Part 1: Multiple choice   8 marks

Mark the appropriate answer (A, B, C or D).

| 0 | A **B** C D |

1	A B C D		5	A B C D
2	A B C D		6	A B C D
3	A B C D		7	A B C D
4	A B C D		8	A B C D

Part 2: Open cloze   8 marks

Write your answers in capital letters, using one box per letter.

| 0 | B | E | C | A | U | S | E | | | |

9.
10.
11.
12.
13.
14.
15.
16.

Bonus material

Part 3: Word formation — 8 marks

Write your answers in capital letters, using one box per letter.

17.
18.
19.
20.
21.
22.
23.
24.

Part 4: Key word transformation — 12 marks

Write your answers in capital letters, using one box per letter.

25.

26.

27.

28.

29.

30.

Cambridge
B2 First
Use of English

Test 3

Cambridge B2 First Use of English

Part 1

For questions 1–8, read the text below and decide which answer best fits each gap. In the separate answer sheet, mark the appropriate answer (A, B, C or D).

Blind football

Football is the world's most popular game, and now 'blind football', also known as 'B1 Football', is starting to **(1)**_____ on globally. Despite its challenges, this game offers excitement, athleticism and teamwork, making it a **(2)**_____ with both players and fans alike.

To play blind football, all players must wear eye masks, ensuring that everyone is on a level playing **(3)**_____. Players must also have a certain level of visual impairment to be **(4)**_____ to play, making the sport inclusive to those with varying degrees of blindness.

The game is played using a special ball that has bells inside. The objective of the game is to score goals by kicking the ball into the opponent's net while **(5)**_____ on the sound of the ball to guide them.

Blind football has been gaining **(6)**_____ in recent years, and it is now played in more than 50 countries. The sport is also achieving recognition at an international level, with the **(7)**_____ of blind football in the Paralympics. In addition, the International Blind Sports Federation governs the sport, ensuring fair play and the **(8)**_____ growth of the game.

1	A	live	B	catch	C	take	D	build
2	A	desire	B	treasure	C	favourite	D	preference
3	A	track	B	pitch	C	field	D	court
4	A	eligible	B	prepared	C	competent	D	deserving
5	A	trusting	B	calculating	C	expecting	D	relying
6	A	validation	B	popularity	C	celebration	D	demand
7	A	instruction	B	immigration	C	identification	D	introduction
8	A	continued	B	remaining	C	extended	D	renewed

Test 3

Part 2

For questions 9–16, read the text below and decide which word best fits each gap. Use only one word for each gap. In the separate answer sheet, write your answers in capital letters, using one box per letter.

Korean street food

Korean street food, with its unique blend of bold and spicy tastes that are unlike anything **(9)**_____, has been taking the world by storm. This delicious cuisine consists of a wide range of dishes that are **(10)**_____ comforting and flavourful, making it a hit in both Europe and the USA.

Korean street food is like a flavour explosion in your mouth, with every bite packed with a bold mix **(11)**_____ sweet, spicy and savoury. The texture of the food **(12)**_____ also a standout feature, with many dishes featuring a crispy and crunchy outer layer that gives way **(13)**_____ a soft and juicy interior.

An all-time classic is Korean fried chicken, which is similar to traditional fried chicken but with **(14)**_____ twist. The crispy skin is coated in a sweet and spicy glaze that packs a flavourful punch, and the chicken itself is tender and juicy, making it a must-try for any foodie.

Or try 'tteokbokki', chewy rice cakes **(15)**_____ are cooked in a spicy and savoury sauce. The dish is often topped **(16)**_____ sliced fish cakes and scallions, adding even more flavour and texture to this delicious treat.

Whether you're a fan of bold and spicy flavours or just looking for a unique culinary experience, Korean street food is definitely worth a try.

Cambridge B2 First Use of English

Part 3

For questions 17–24, use the stem word on the right to form the correct word that fills each gap. In the separate answer sheet, write your answers in capital letters, using one box per letter.

Emergency aid

In times of crisis, emergency aid can mean the difference between life and death for those **(17)**_____. People are often amazed by how quickly NGOs are able to get up and running within a matter of days of a disaster. Although it's impossible to prepare for any specific emergency, we do have plans in place that **(18)**_____ us to get moving quickly.

AFFECT

ABLE

If you're wondering how we provide emergency aid to local **(19)**_____ during a crisis, here is our approach.

RESIDE

Most importantly, act fast: In a crisis, every second counts. Timing is **(20)**_____ when it comes to providing emergency aid, aid delays can have dire consequences.

ESSENCE

When **(21)**_____ emergency aid, it's crucial to listen to the needs of those who have been hard hit. This includes understanding the specific challenges they face, and adapting aid efforts **(22)**_____. Do people need water, shelter, medicine – or all three?

SUPPLY

ACCORD

Hand out aid quickly and effectively: Once the aid has been gathered, it's important that it's not distributed in an **(23)**_____ way. This includes prioritizing the most critical situations, and **(24)**_____ that resources don't run out.

EFFICIENT
SURE

By following these steps, we can work together to provide emergency aid during times of crisis and help people to recover and rebuild.

Test 3

Part 4

For questions 25–30, complete the second sentence, using the word given, so that it has a similar meaning to the first sentence. Do not change the word provided and use between two and five words in total. In the separate answer sheet, write your answers in capital letters, using one box per letter.

25 "Luca's really disappointed everyone in the team," said the manager.
    LET
    The manager said that Luca had really _____.

26 He didn't try to be friendly with the new student.
    MADE
    He _____ effort to be kind to the new student.

27 The students began to move slowly out of the hall.
    WAY
    The students slowly _____ out of the hall.

28 When we were kids we went to the beach every weekend.
    WOULD
    As kids _____ to the beach at weekends.

29 I shouldn't have gone to bed so late last night.
    WISH
    I _____ gone to bed so late last night.

30 Hurry up, our train will be leaving in a few minutes.
    ABOUT
    We need to hurry, our train _____ leave.

Cambridge B2 First Use of English

Answer sheet: Cambridge B2 First Use of English

Test No. ☐

Mark out of 36 ☐

Name _____ Date _____

Part 1: Multiple choice

8 marks

Mark the appropriate answer (A, B, C or D).

| 0 | A | **B** | C | D |

1	A	B	C	D
2	A	B	C	D
3	A	B	C	D
4	A	B	C	D

5	A	B	C	D
6	A	B	C	D
7	A	B	C	D
8	A	B	C	D

Part 2: Open cloze

8 marks

Write your answers in capital letters, using one box per letter.

| 0 | B | E | C | A | U | S | E | | | |

9.
10.
11.
12.
13.
14.
15.
16.

Part 3: Word formation 8 marks

Write your answers in capital letters, using one box per letter.

17.
18.
19.
20.
21.
22.
23.
24.

Part 4: Key word transformation 12 marks

Write your answers in capital letters, using one box per letter.

25.

26.

27.

28.

29.

30.

Notes

www.ingramcontent.com/pod-product-compliance
Lightning Source LLC
Chambersburg PA
CBHW081918090526
44590CB00019B/3399